LIGHT AFTER LIGHT

Victoria Gatehouse was born in Leeds, and now lives in the West Yorkshire village of Ripponden with her family. She is a clinical researcher with an MA in Creative Writing from MMU. Her work has been widely published in magazines and anthologies including *Magma, Mslexia, The North, The Rialto, Her Wings of Glass* (Second Light Publications, 2014) and *The Emma Press Anthology of Mildly Erotic Verse* (The Emma Press, 2013). Competition wins include Ilkley, PENfro and the Poetry News Members' Competition, and she has been placed in many more. In 2016, she was shortlisted for the Flambard Poetry Prize.

# Light After Light

VICTORIA GATEHOUSE

**VP**

*Valley Press*

First published in 2018 by Valley Press
Woodend, The Crescent, Scarborough, YO11 2PW
www.valleypressuk.com

First edition, first printing (March 2018)

ISBN 978-1-908853-97-4
Cat. no. VP0114

Copyright © Victoria Gatehouse 2018

The right of Victoria Gatehouse to be identified as the author of this work has been asserted in accordance with the Copyright, Designs and Patents Act 1988.

All rights reserved. No part of this publication may be reproduced, stored in or introduced into a retrieval system, or transmitted in any form, by any means (electronic, mechanical, photocopying, recording or otherwise) without prior written permission from the rights holders.

A CIP record for this book is available from the British Library.

Cover design by Jamie McGarry. Text design by Jo Haywood.

Printed and bound in Great Britain by
Imprint Digital, Upton Pyne, Exeter.

# Contents

Power Cut  9
Blackpool  10
Turbines  12
Hymn for the Ash  13
Brace  14
Phosphorescence  15
Flame Test  16
The Geese of Sowerby Bridge  18
The Moth  19
In Praise of Pylons  20
Turnout  22
Little Red  23
Burning Mouth Syndrome  24
Widow  25
Velvet Shells  26
Pillion  28
Weathering the Tent  30
Recording the Phlebotomist  32
The Summer Queen  33
Where the Snow Stays  34

# Acknowledgements

Versions of these poems have appeared in: *Her Wings of Glass* (Second Light Publications), *Ink Sweat and Tears*, *Mslexia*, *Pennine Platform*, *Poetry News*, *Prole*, *The Chronicles of Eve* (Paper Swans Press), *The Emma Press Anthology of Mildly Erotic Verse*, *The Flambard Prizewinners' Anthology 2016*, *The Interpreter's House*, *The North*, *An Anthology of Urban Legend and Modern Folklore* (Three Drops Press) and *The Telegraph*.

'Power Cut' was a winner in the *Poetry News* Members' Competition, 2015. 'In Praise of Pylons' won the 2011 Ilkley Literature Festival Poetry Prize.

Poems in this pamphlet have also been placed in the following open poetry competitions: Mslexia Single Poem; Prole Laureate; Poetry on the Lake; The Interpreter's House Competition; and Wordpool Poetry Prize.

Sincere thanks to Sally Baker for her invaluable editorial assistance. Also to Keith Hutson, the tutors at MMU, Sarah Corbett, Wendy Pratt, John Foggin, Catherine Smith, the wonderful Hebden Bridge 'Caldergate' group and Hope Street Poets, who offered so much useful feedback.

I am deeply indebted to Gaia Holmes and Ann and Peter Sansom for their workshops, which inspired many of these poems. I am grateful to Jamie McGarry and Jo Haywood at Valley Press for publishing this pamphlet, to John for his unwavering support and to my family and friends for encouraging and believing in me.

*'Don't tell me the moon is shining; show me the glint of light on broken glass.'*

ANTON CHEKHOV

# Power Cut

You strike the first match –
the room lurches
from black to indistinct

before colour reasserts itself
in ambers and golds.

Walls and ceilings shift and dip,
all down the street
windows flickering,

half the valley out by the look of it
and your face, as you reach

for the corkscrew, is like it was
before the lines crept in,
all the rough edges blurring.

We're adrift, you and I
in aureoles of light, and then

the splutter and fizz
of overhead strips, the glare
of electricals back on again,

your fingers sliding from mine
to nip out all the little flames.

# Blackpool

A week in a guest house, cheap rate;
February lingers like an ache
that can't be slept off. Tonight

you walk the promenade,
the sea black and glittering,
keeper of those things it offered up

back in seventy-nine –
a cache of shells, the empty
breast-plate of a crab, a pebble

shaped like a heart
to be kept in your pocket for luck
or so your father said.

He paid for two weeks every summer,
even in the teenage years
when the arcades drew you in

with their promise of heat and noise
and a jackpot with the next coin.
Remember how you snuck out to meet

that lad who worked the waltzers?
Your father said he was a bad lot
and no doubt he was right –

his Best Lass, with a pebble
like a heart in her pocket, spun
and spun again, in a flurry of lights.

Beneath your coat, he's nothing but ashes.
You keep on – past the pier,
the chippies, the Pleasure Beach.

Before the sea takes him,
the rattle of a Big Dipper
carrying nothing but the stars.

# Turbines

There is so much grace
in their blades.
On idle days

they gleam
like wing bones
of geese, picked clean.

Yet the sun
leaves them cold.
Wait, wait for the wind

and you'll hear them sing,
wheel and whirr
like butchers' machines.

Imagine them
unyoked, freewheeling
across the moors

reeling in the sky
as birds cling
to glittering arcs of air,

resist the pull
of the cutting edge.
Turbines and birds –

their bones so brittle
you could snap
a wish out of them.

# Hymn for the Ash

After the force of the axe,
the honey-bleed,
you will come new again
that green-flame tug

curl into heartwood,
limbs sap-sticky, skin
like lichen plaques,
the whisper of sugar water

inside phloem. Of late
the wind carries a taint,
a canker in the stalks
of last year's fallen leaves.

Spring brings leaf-light
to the woodland floor,
explosions of flowers –
dog violets, garlic,

fruit clusters on twigs;
your own buds fist tight,
full summer before
your brown-wilt crown

turns to the light, a planet
half-blasted, leaning into its sun.

# Brace

At first, snapping on its tightness
she could only manage soup, mashed potato,

pureed fruit, using forefinger and thumb
to ease it out and clean it afterwards

the way she'd been shown, extracting stray pips,
tomato flesh snagged in the gaps.

It was only after the pinch lessened
she progressed to roasties, gravied beef.

But never apples. The dentist said they could break
wires, the skins of Golden Delicious, Cox's;

getting her teeth into them a secret thing
like kissing lads at parties, that trick

of turning her face away, fingers quick
on the plate, the slick transfer of brace

to pocket, tongue over teeth to remove any bits
and then sneaking into bathrooms afterwards,

the rush of water over metal before clicking
it back into place, the ache of something moving

and her tongue unable to leave it alone.

# Phosphorescence

*Record this* you say and I'm left
in the shallows, holding your phone.

And I capture it all – the moon
low and lush as a forbidden fruit,

you, striking light after light
as you cross the bay; the way

your face, as you turn to wave,
is star-varnished like that of a god.

Before you upload, before the flurry
of *likes* for this phenomenon,

there's a moment when your world
is gleaming in my hands. Tonight

I would gulp down this blooming ocean
for a taste of your skin.

# Flame Test

We swapped lab partners every term;
once, in Lower Sixth, I paired up

with Scott Wainwright. Neither of us
spoke as I elastic-banded my hair,

fumbled with vinyl gloves
before un-stoppering

the sulphuric acid, which fumed
so we leapt back, almost

shared a laugh. Then I dipped
the nichrome loop while his inky fingers

flicked air valves closed,
turned the Bunsen blue. He gave me

goggles and the briefest of glances
through reinforced plastic

before I edged the loop
into the hottest place, held steady

until it burned clear
enough for testing to begin.

Metal after metal we put through
that flame, noting down shifts

in colour; some seeming to merge
into one another, others feeding

the tip of the next, none of them
a textbook match. After we

guessed number six to be lithium,
he said I could call him

Wainy if I liked and the teacher,
she said it was the basis for fireworks.

## The Geese of Sowerby Bridge

You'll see them patrolling the High Street –
ganging up on the corner by *The Long Chimney*,
intimidating passers-by with a show
of downy muscle, a half-lift of wings,

causing tail backs when they choose
to cross the road, a twenty-strong gaggle
impervious to hoots. And always a straggler
who'll pause to shit before reaching the verge.

The *Courier* receives a letter a week
citing *dangerous droppings* and *a town invaded*
and councillors have put up a *Please Do Not Feed*
but there are plenty who bring bread

only to find themselves surrounded,
held hostage by a scrabble of beaks and wings,
the geese strutting bolshie, hissy fitting
on the tarmac like girls fresh from *Roxy*.

Once I walked the canal path in March,
caught them inching down the banks of the Calder,
webbed feet side-stepping takeaway boxes,
Strongbow cans, netting cast out from factory yards,

the females lifting the strong, pale curves
of their necks as they settled on nests
that held the fluttering scraps of plastic bags,
the glitter of broken glass.

## The Moth

This is her time –
birds dark-stitching telegraph wires,

the woods blue-shadowed,
crackling with dusk.

The moon untethers her,
she pitches from fence to wall

to leaf, would hurl herself
for miles, such is her faith.

You think of how she gorged
on hawthorn and thyme, spun

herself a mantle, hung tight
inside the blackout

of her own skin
before the breakdown, the forcing

of all that remained
through the veins of her wings,

this lit-bulb junkie,
wrecking herself on your porch light.

# In Praise of Pylons

Sometimes I think of the pylons,
so ubiquitous we tune out

their dark glower over moorland
motorway and housing estate,

move unseeing beneath
massive steel shoulders

that never sag
from the weight of the Grid.

These are lonely Stoics,
their fate to hold

the power, yet never to feel
electrons leap

through the wires that hang
from wrist to twisted wrist.

To those who would brand them
as eyesores, I say only this –

if you took the time
you'd look up to them as more

than harbingers of light and tea
and your favourite soap;

the dying sun
worships the bones of them

and hurricanes can't shake free
the diamonds that make up their core

and if you take
the path beneath the power lines

on a day when the rain offers up
beads on the wire

your hair might lift
as though at the swell of a choir.

## Turnout

Unexpected, this white-knuckled lawn,
this leather-capped cluster
beneath the trees, soft pleats of gills
surfacing from deadwood,

roly-poly bodies sponging
off the rain and it's the thought
of what they could be that holds you
in your dressing gown still

on a damp October lunchtime –
*saffron milkcups, chanterelles,*
*destroying angels, slippery jacks.*
Theirs, a poetry that fruits on decay

slides through the lips
promising raw meat or silk
and you'll savour it slow,
this bellyful of possibility and rot.

# Little Red

So much has been said of me,
the girl in the red velvet cap
with her basket of cake and wine –
*so sweet, so kind.*

You think I wanted
that do-gooder woodcutter
to snip open the wolf?

It was dark in there,
so magnificently dark,
all the better to hear
the surge of his heart
through artery and valve.

And I would have stayed,
would have raged through his blood
like a blizzard, clawed my fingers
into the pads of his paws,

his pelt, a hand-me-down coat,
his mouth, my mouth, dripping
from the last kill,
not knowing when or how

to stop, only that to remain
on this path, collecting stones,
would be the worst kind of death.

# Burning Mouth Syndrome

The doctor says it's nothing serious, something
she'll just have to live with, a malfunction
of the nerves perhaps, not uncommon in women of her age
and she leaves with a script for a mild antidepressant,
a leaflet counselling moderation in alcohol, tobacco
and spicy foods and when she returns, he says it again
after taking a look at lips, teeth and tongue –
'nothing to see' and he says it with a smile when she can feel
the bees humming in her blood, the tips of their wings
chafing artery walls and she knows without being told
they're house bees, the ones who feed, clean
and ventilate the hive, pack nectar into the comb
without really tasting it, the ones who wait for mid-life
to take their first orientation flights and she can really
feel the smart of them, the bees in her blood, unfurling
their proboscises to touch the corolla of her heart.
So many years spent licking out hives, all the burn of it
here on her tongue and they're starting to forage now,
to suck sweetness into their honey stomachs, and the doctor,
he'll keep telling her it's nothing as they rise
like stings, the words she's kept in.

# Widow

*Following the death of her husband, artist Susie MacMurray*
*created a dress made entirely of pins.*

You'll find me glittering in doorways,
waiting, like a bride, to snag everyone's eye.

As a bride, I stood through countless fittings,
knew the hopeful calculations of the measuring tape.

Now I've taken shears to dreams, watched beads
of blood swell and break on the fingertips

of those who re-stitched the seams. Watch me
thread my way across the room. In my wake

a shivering train, the clicking grief
of one hundred thousand adamantine pins.

From a distance, they're glossy with light,
lie like a pelt. Touchable. Come closer –

held in the smooth weight of each head,
a fleck of memory, the tight edge of a tear.

# Velvet Shells

*In one of her installations, artist Susie MacMurray
lined mussel shells with velvet.*

They've passed the test –
that tap from Chef's blade,
a glimmer of muscle

from those still alive
before the pile-up,
blue and black

on a white plate.
She imagines lovers
scooping out

wine-soaked flesh,
that slow contraction
of spirits in the throat;

on the side, a stack
of coffins, unhinged.
She's a collector

of leftovers,
a scavenger
of restaurant bins.

All the way home
that rattle in her hands
and afterwards

hours of scrubbing
the shine back in,
before laying them out

with such care
on the kitchen table,
folding crimson velvet

into emptiness,
offering up a prayer
for every little death.

# Pillion

It was the friend of your brother's friend
who picked her up that night,

a skin of ice on the bypass
causing him to slow, to catch

the pale billow of her hair
as she waited on the hard shoulder,

crash helmet removed, thumbing for a lift.
When he swerved, pulled over on a scream

of brakes, she stood as if frozen,
unblinking as a wild animal in his lights.

The whisper of an address, cold
against his cheek, a creak of leather

and she's riding pillion, leaning
into the bends like his shadow-self

and there's that moment when he glances
behind him and she's not there.

It goes without saying, he reported
the incident to the police,

visited her house to find the girl
was killed a month ago

on that same stretch of road.
The friend of your brother's friend,

he won't ride that way again
for fear she'll slip in behind him, the girl

who travelled so light he could barely
feel her fingers at his waist.

# Weathering the Tent

Tonight, we pack up the tent –
a corner at a time, our familiar routine, folding
the canvas we weathered twenty years ago,
cocooned in green dimness, listening, listening
until finally, that drip drip drip on our faces
as we lay on the groundsheet, numb-backed
from the cold, every one of your roll-ups
lighting me up, a catch in my throat;
over our heads that slow expansion,
fibres growing into one another,
meshing until watertight.
Tonight, kneeling side by side,
we press forward to quash the billow,
releasing breaths of earth, smoke, gabardine.
All creaking resistance, this fabric,
you and I cursing, our guy-roped hands
holding out for old creases.
All these years of practice and still
so many attempts
to force another summer into the bag.

To force another summer into the bag –
so many attempts,
all these years of practice and still
holding out for old creases;
you and I cursing, our guy-roped hands
all creaking resistance, this fabric
releasing breaths of earth, smoke, gabardine.
We press forward to quash the billow
tonight, kneeling side by side
meshing until watertight,
fibres growing into one another;
over our heads that slow expansion
lighting me up, a catch in my throat
from the cold, every one of your roll-ups,
as we lay on the groundsheet, numb-backed,
until finally, that drip, drip, drip on our faces.
Cocooned in green dimness, listening, listening –
the canvas we weathered twenty years ago,
a corner at a time, our familiar routine, folding.
Tonight, we pack up the tent.

# Recording the Phlebotomist

*'Please do not attempt to photograph or record
any part of the phlebotomy process'
(Notice at Huddersfield Royal Infirmary)*

He informs me, very politely
that he's going to take my blood,
this pale young man in his disposable apron.
I suppose I could, at this point
take out my phone to record
his newly-disinfected hands twist
the tourniquet tight, delicate fingers
flicking the inside of my elbow
in exactly the right place to summon
the blue. And perhaps a still
of that precise moment when the needle breaks
the surface or the opportunity
to replay in slow motion, the draw,
the smooth filling of the tube,
remembering the sting, the velvet heat.
Afterwards I might decide to zoom in
on my own fingers pressing the swab
as he withdraws, *hold still, careful now*
before moving out of shot to label the vial,
tipping to mix my dark red cells. But then
there's only one part I want to recall,
his voice: *you've got lovely veins.*

# The Summer Queen

They've decked her out in Christmas lights –
a bobbing string, from mast to stern.
Each snap of wind's a switch – unlit to lit
these bulbs, their pale hearts failing
to brighten a harbour where granite waves
roll themselves from wall to wall
and locals pass, heads bowed,
unmoved by the Rudolph flag,
or Santa, roped to the prow,
his gait the lurch of the half-inflated.

But someone will come,
a day-tripper perhaps, willing to pay
three quid for a 'Pleasure Cruise',
the offer of a blue padded seat
in a covered saloon and a view to look back on –
the lean, tarnished ribs of the pier,
cottages, slope-stacked on cliffs,
the lights of Whitby, receding

taking on the cold distance of stars
as an ocean opens up
and the skipper, eyes to the horizon,
tells tales of September shoals, swift glints
of mackerel and herring, the dark cut
of minke fins in their wake.

# Where the Snow Stays

Days after thaw waters cease to rush
beneath the grid at the end of the lane

and the dam's frozen tongue comes unstuck,
a stained crust remains on the edge of the drive

it took you a morning to clear, a tyre's brand
marks the verge where you failed to turn.

And after the snow ploughs and gritters
have passed, the moors' hunched backs

retain seams of white. You come to know
the shapes of them, these snow-fossils –

the gleam of a rib, the splintered ridge
of a clavicle, the shrinking plates of a spine,

will carry their imprint long after
the rains sweep in, dissolving

the marrow, making the heather shine.